I0477860

Table of Contents

Introduction

Welcome to "The Ultimate Guide on How to Start a Fractional COO Business," a comprehensive resource designed to provide entrepreneurs like you with the knowledge and strategies needed to launch a successful fractional COO business. This book will guide you step-by-step through the process of starting and growing your own business, from assessing your skills and experience to managing and scaling your operations.

Chapter 1: Introduction to Fractional COO Services

In this chapter, we will explore the concept of fractional COO services and why it has become an increasingly popular option for businesses of all sizes. We'll discuss the responsibilities and benefits of hiring a fractional COO, as well as the unique value they bring to an organization. You'll learn how fractional COOs can help businesses streamline operations, improve efficiency, and drive growth.

Chapter 2: Assessing Your Skills and Experience

Before diving into the world of fractional COO services, it's essential to assess your skills, experience, and qualifications. This chapter will guide you through a self-assessment process, helping you determine if you possess the necessary expertise and traits to succeed in this field. We will also discuss the importance of continuous learning and professional development in enhancing your capabilities as a fractional COO.

Chapter 3: Understanding the Role of a Fractional COO

To effectively offer fractional COO services, you must have a thorough understanding of the role you will be playing within an organization. This chapter will delve into the various responsibilities, duties, and expectations that come with being a fractional COO. From strategic planning and operational management to team leadership and problem-solving, we will explore the different facets of this pivotal role.

Chapter 4: Setting Up Your Fractional COO Business

Once you have assessed your skills and gained a clear understanding of the fractional COO role, it's time to set up your own business. This chapter will provide you with practical guidance on establishing a legal entity, creating a business plan, and setting up essential infrastructure such as a website, office space, and technology systems. We will also discuss the importance of building a brand

and developing a marketing strategy to attract potential clients.

Chapter 5: Building Your Client Base

In this chapter, we will explore effective strategies for finding and acquiring clients for your fractional COO services. From networking and referrals to online marketing and social media presence, we will provide you with actionable tips on building a robust client base. Additionally, we will discuss the significance of maintaining strong relationships with existing clients to foster loyalty and encourage referrals.

Chapter 6: Providing Exceptional Fractional COO Services

Delivering exceptional fractional COO services is crucial for building a strong reputation and ensuring client satisfaction. This chapter will focus on the strategies and techniques you can employ to provide exceptional services to your clients. We will cover effective communication, problem-solving skills, and the importance of adapting to different organizational cultures and contexts.

Chapter 7: Pricing Your Fractional COO Services

Determining the right pricing strategy is essential in running a successful fractional

COO business. This chapter will guide you through the process of pricing your services, taking into account factors such as your experience, the value you provide, and the market demand. We will explore different pricing models and discuss the importance of flexibility and transparency in your pricing structure.

Chapter 8: Managing Your Fractional COO Business

Managing your fractional COO business effectively is crucial for long-term success. In this chapter, we will delve into various key aspects of business management, including financial management, client relationship management, and team building. We will discuss how to streamline your operations, leverage technology, and build a strong support network to ensure the smooth running of your business.

Chapter 9: Scaling Your Fractional COO Business

Scaling your fractional COO business allows you to expand your reach and increase your impact. This chapter will explore different strategies and considerations for scaling your operations, such as hiring additional team members, diversifying your service offerings, and targeting new markets. We will also discuss the importance of creating systems and processes to maintain consistency and efficiency as your business grows.

Chapter 10: Navigating Challenges and Sustaining Success

Building and sustaining a successful fractional COO business comes with its own set of challenges. In this final chapter, we will discuss common obstacles you may encounter along the way and provide strategies for overcoming them. Topics will include dealing with difficult clients, managing time effectively, and staying motivated and resilient in the face of adversity. Additionally, we will explore how to continually evolve, innovate, and adapt to stay ahead in the ever-changing business landscape.

With each chapter, you will gain valuable insights, practical tips, and actionable steps to help you navigate the exciting journey of starting and growing your own fractional COO business. Let's embark on this adventure together and empower you to create a thriving and impactful business.

Chapter 1: Introduction to Fractional COO Services

Fractional Chief Operating Officer (COO) services have become increasingly popular among businesses in recent years. As an entrepreneur, it's crucial to understand the role and potential benefits of hiring a Fractional COO for your organization. In this chapter, we'll dive deeper into the concept of Fractional COO services and explore how they can help businesses thrive.

What are Fractional COO Services?

Fractional COO services involve hiring a part-time or temporary Chief Operating Officer to assist in managing the day-to-day operations of a business. Unlike a full-time COO, a Fractional COO provides their expertise on a project basis or for a designated period. This flexible arrangement allows businesses to access high-level strategic guidance and operational support without the need for a long-term commitment.

The Benefits of Fractional COO Services

There are several advantages to hiring a Fractional COO for your business:

Cost Efficiency:

1. Fractional COOs offer their services on a contractual basis, allowing businesses to access top-level executive talent at a fraction of the cost of hiring a full-time COO. This cost-effective solution is particularly beneficial for startups and small businesses with limited financial resources.

Expertise and Experience:

2. Fractional COOs bring a wealth of expertise and experience to the table. They have typically held high-level executive positions in various industries and possess a deep understanding of business operations. Their knowledge can help streamline processes, optimize productivity, and drive growth for your organization.

Objective Perspective:

3. An external Fractional COO provides an objective viewpoint, free from internal biases and politics. They can identify inefficiencies, bottlenecks, and areas for improvement that may go unnoticed by in-house staff. This fresh perspective can lead to innovative solutions and improved decision-making.

Scalability:

4. As your business evolves, so do its operational needs. Fractional COOs offer scalability by adjusting their level of involvement based on your business requirements. Whether you need temporary support during a growth phase or specific expertise for a particular project, a Fractional COO can adapt to your changing needs.

Is a Fractional COO Right for Your Business?

While Fractional COO services offer numerous benefits, it's essential to evaluate whether this arrangement aligns with your business goals and requirements. Consider the following factors:

- The complexity of your operations and the need for strategic guidance.
- Your budget limitations and the feasibility of hiring a full-time COO.
- The scale of your business and its potential for growth.
- The specific expertise and experience required to address your operational challenges.

In the subsequent chapters, we will explore how to assess your skills and experience in becoming a Fractional COO, the role and responsibilities of a Fractional COO, setting up your Fractional COO business, and much more. By the end of this book, you will have gained the knowledge and insights needed to embark on your entrepreneurial journey as a Fractional COO and provide exceptional services to your clients.

By understanding the ins and outs of Fractional COO services, you'll be better equipped to decide if this flexible and strategic approach is right for your business. As you continue through this book, you'll discover how to effectively leverage a Fractional COO to optimize your operations and drive your business toward sustained success.

Chapter 2: Assessing Your Skills and Experience

As you consider starting your own fractional COO business, it's crucial to assess your skills and experience to determine if you have what it takes to excel in this role. Being a successful fractional COO requires a combination of leadership, strategic thinking, and operational expertise. Let's delve into each of these areas and see how you can evaluate your readiness for this exciting venture.

Evaluating Your Leadership Abilities

Leadership is a fundamental skill for a COO, regardless of whether they are full-time or fractional. As a fractional COO, you will be responsible for guiding and inspiring teams, driving organizational change, and making critical decisions to achieve business objectives. Reflecting on your previous leadership experiences can help you gauge your readiness. Here are some questions to consider:

Have you held leadership positions in the past? Think about any management roles you've had, whether in a professional setting or even in volunteer capacities. Leadership is about more than just titles; it's about the impact you've had on others. Did you successfully lead a project or a team? How did you handle challenges and setbacks? Your past experiences can provide valuable insights into your leadership capabilities.

How well do you communicate and collaborate with others?
Effective communication and collaboration are essential for a fractional COO. You will need to work closely with the business owner and other stakeholders to align strategies, define goals, and ensure smooth operations. Consider how well you've managed relationships and communication in your previous roles. Have you been able to convey your ideas clearly and work well with diverse teams?

Are you comfortable making tough decisions? Fractional COOs often encounter complex situations that require quick decision-making. Assess your ability to handle high-pressure scenarios and make informed choices. Think about times when you've had to make difficult decisions. How did you approach the situation? What was the outcome? Your ability to stay calm and decisive under pressure is crucial for this role.

Assessing Your Strategic Thinking Skills

Strategic thinking is another key competency for a fractional COO. As a strategic partner to the business owner, you will be responsible for developing and executing plans to drive growth and improve operational efficiency. Here are some points to consider when evaluating your strategic thinking skills:

How well do you understand the business landscape?
To effectively contribute as a fractional COO, you need to have a deep understanding of the industry, market trends, and the competitive landscape. Reflect on your knowledge of the industry you're targeting. Do you keep up with the latest trends and developments? Can you anticipate changes and adapt your strategies accordingly?

Can you analyze complex problems and develop innovative solutions?
Fractional COOs are often called upon to solve difficult challenges. Assess your ability to analyze complex problems, think critically, and develop innovative solutions. Think about a time when you faced a particularly tough problem. How did you break it down and find a solution? Your problem-solving skills are a vital asset in this role.

Are you skilled at translating strategic goals into actionable plans?
As a fractional COO, you will need to convert high-level strategic goals into practical and achievable action plans. Evaluate your capability to create detailed plans that align with the overall business strategy. Consider your experience in project management and execution. Can you take a broad vision and break it down into manageable steps?

Evaluating Your Operational Expertise

Operational expertise is another crucial aspect of being a fractional COO. You need to have a strong background in operational management to identify areas for improvement, optimize processes, and drive efficiency within the organization. Here are some factors to consider when assessing your operational expertise:

What is your experience in managing business operations?
Reflect on your previous roles and responsibilities related to operational management. Consider the scope and complexity of the operations you have overseen. Have you managed day-to-day operations, optimized processes, or implemented new systems? Your hands-on

experience will be key to your success as a fractional COO.

Are you familiar with the latest industry best practices?
Staying up to date with the latest industry trends and best practices is essential for a fractional COO. Evaluate your knowledge in areas such as project management, supply chain optimization, and organizational design. How proactive are you in continuing your education and staying current with industry standards?

Do you possess a strong attention to detail?
Operational excellence often requires meticulous attention to detail. Assess your ability to identify and address operational inefficiencies and implement improvements. Think about your past work. Were you able to spot issues before they became problems? How did you ensure that operations ran smoothly?

Conclusion

Assessing your skills and experience is a critical step in determining if you are well-equipped to start a fractional COO business. Leadership abilities, strategic thinking skills, and operational expertise are all vital for success in this role. Take the time to reflect on your strengths and areas for development. By doing so, you can ensure you're prepared to provide exceptional fractional COO services to your future clients. This self-assessment will not only help you identify your readiness but also highlight areas where you may need to grow or seek additional training. Remember, the journey to becoming a successful fractional COO is ongoing, and continuous improvement is key.

Chapter 3: Understanding the Role of a Fractional COO

As an entrepreneur considering starting a fractional COO business, it's crucial to have a clear and thorough understanding of what the role entails. In this chapter, we'll delve into the responsibilities and functions of a fractional COO, giving you a comprehensive overview of what you need to know.

The Role of a Fractional COO

A fractional COO, sometimes called a part-time or temporary Chief Operating Officer, is a professional who provides strategic guidance and operational support to businesses on a fractional basis. They work closely with the leadership team and other key stakeholders to drive efficiency, improve processes, and ensure the smooth functioning of the organization. This role is versatile and adaptable, making it an invaluable asset to businesses of all sizes.

Strategic Planning and Execution

One of the primary responsibilities of a fractional COO is to assist the business in developing and executing its strategic plan. They collaborate with the CEO or business owner to define the company's goals, long-term vision, and growth strategies. By leveraging their expertise, the fractional COO helps translate strategic objectives into actionable plans and ensures proper execution throughout the organization.

For example, if a company aims to expand its market presence, the fractional COO might develop a detailed expansion plan that includes market research, resource allocation, and a timeline for implementation. They then work with various departments to ensure that each step of the plan is carried out effectively.

Operational Management

Managing day-to-day operations is a critical part of a fractional COO's role. They oversee various functional areas, ensuring that each department aligns with the overall business objectives. From optimizing processes and streamlining workflows to implementing effective systems and technologies, fractional COOs work to improve operational efficiency and maximize productivity.

Imagine a scenario where a business struggles with inefficiencies in its production line. A fractional COO would analyze the current processes, identify bottlenecks, and implement solutions to streamline operations. This could involve introducing new technologies, reorganizing workflows, or training staff on best practices.

Financial Management

Another essential aspect of the fractional COO's role is financial management. They collaborate with the finance team to develop budgets, financial forecasts, and performance metrics. By monitoring key financial indicators, analyzing trends, and identifying areas for improvement, they help drive financial stability and profitability.

For instance, a fractional COO might work with the finance team to create a budget that supports the company's strategic goals while ensuring financial prudence. They might also implement performance metrics to track progress and adjust strategies as needed to stay on course.

Team Leadership and Development

Leading and developing teams is a fundamental responsibility of a fractional COO.

They work closely with department heads to assess staffing needs, recruit top talent, and foster a high-performance culture. By providing guidance, mentorship, and professional development opportunities, the fractional COO ensures that the organization has a skilled and motivated workforce.

Consider a company aiming to improve its employee retention rates. A fractional COO might implement leadership development programs, create mentorship opportunities, and foster a culture of continuous improvement to keep employees engaged and committed to the organization.

Change Management

In a business landscape that is constantly evolving, adaptability and change management skills are crucial. Fractional COOs assist businesses in navigating change by evaluating current processes, identifying areas of improvement, and implementing necessary changes. They help manage organizational transitions smoothly, minimizing disruptions and maximizing the chances of success.

For example, if a company is merging with another, a fractional COO would oversee the integration process, ensuring that systems and cultures merge seamlessly. They might facilitate communication between teams, align goals, and address any resistance to change.

Relationship Management

Developing and maintaining strong relationships with key stakeholders is a fundamental aspect of a fractional COO's role. They collaborate with clients, vendors, and partners, ensuring effective communication and fostering mutually beneficial partnerships. Additionally, fractional COOs work closely with the leadership team to build a culture of collaboration and transparency within the organization.

For instance, a fractional COO might negotiate with key suppliers to secure better terms, or they might work with clients to understand their needs better and tailor services accordingly.

Understanding the multifaceted role of a fractional COO is essential when starting your own fractional COO business. A fractional COO brings strategic thinking, operational expertise, and leadership skills to help businesses thrive. By offering a comprehensive range of services, you can become a valuable asset to organizations seeking part-time or temporary executive-level support.

In the next chapter, we'll explore how to set up your fractional COO business, providing you with practical steps and insights to get started on the right foot. Let's continue this journey together and equip you with the tools you need for success.

Chapter 4: Setting Up Your Fractional COO Business

Starting a fractional COO business is an exciting venture that requires careful planning and preparation. In this chapter, we'll guide you through the essential steps needed to set up a successful fractional COO business. Let's dive into the details and ensure you're well-prepared for your entrepreneurial journey.

1. Define Your Business Structure

The first step in setting up your fractional COO business is determining the legal structure of your company. You have several options, including operating as a sole proprietorship, a partnership, a limited liability company (LLC), or a corporation. Each structure has its own advantages and considerations.

- **Sole Proprietorship:** This is the simplest structure, where you and the business are legally the same. It's easy to set up but doesn't offer liability protection.
- **Partnership:** If you plan to start the business with someone else, a

partnership might be suitable. It involves shared ownership and responsibilities.
- **LLC:** This structure provides liability protection without the complexity of a corporation. It's a popular choice for small businesses.
- **Corporation:** This is more complex and suited for larger businesses with significant growth potential. It offers liability protection and can attract investors.

Research each option and select the one that best aligns with your business goals and needs.

2. Register Your Business

Once you've decided on a business structure, the next step is to register your fractional COO business with the appropriate government authorities. This typically involves filing the necessary paperwork and paying registration fees.

- **Choose a Business Name:** Make sure it's unique and reflects your services.
- **File Registration Documents:** Depending on your chosen structure, this could be a simple form or more detailed articles of incorporation.

- **Obtain an EIN:** An Employer Identification Number (EIN) is like a social security number for your business. It's required for tax purposes.

Consult with a lawyer or business advisor to ensure you comply with all legal requirements in your jurisdiction.

3. Obtain the Required Licenses and Permits

Depending on your location and the services you plan to offer, you may need certain licenses or permits to operate your fractional COO business legally.

- **Research Local Regulations:** Check with local, state, and federal agencies to determine the specific licenses and permits you may need.
- **Industry-Specific Licenses:** Some industries require professional certifications or specific licenses.

Ensuring you have all the necessary documentation will help you avoid legal issues and establish credibility with clients.

4. Set Up Your Workspace and Equipment

Creating a conducive workspace is crucial to the success of your fractional COO business. Here's how to get started:

- **Dedicated Office Space:** Whether it's a home office or a rented space, make sure it's free from distractions and conducive to productivity.
- **Essential Tools and Equipment:** Invest in a reliable computer, phone system, high-speed internet connection, and office supplies.
- **Technology:** Consider project management software (like Asana or Trello), communication tools (like Slack), and other technology that will help you manage your clients and projects efficiently.

5. Develop a Marketing Strategy

To attract clients and establish your presence in the market, you need a comprehensive marketing strategy:

- **Identify Your Target Audience:** Understand their needs and pain points.
- **Create a Compelling Brand Identity:** Develop a professional website that showcases your expertise and the value you can bring to clients.

- **Utilize Marketing Channels:** Use social media, content marketing, networking events, and industry conferences to raise awareness of your fractional COO services.

6. Build a Network

Building a strong network is vital for the success of your fractional COO business. Here's how to expand your connections:

- **Connect with Industry Professionals:** Attend networking events, join industry associations, and engage in online forums.
- **Establish Yourself as a Thought Leader:** Participate in discussions, share insights, and contribute valuable content to build relationships with potential clients and partners.

7. Develop Service Offerings and Pricing Structure

Define the specific services you will offer as a fractional COO and determine a pricing structure that reflects the value you bring to clients. Consider the following:

- **Services:** Decide whether you'll offer strategic planning, process optimization,

team management, or other operational support.
- **Pricing:** Consider your experience level, project complexity, and market rates. Be transparent about your pricing and clearly communicate the benefits clients can expect.

8. Create Contracts and Agreements

Protect yourself and your clients by creating clear and comprehensive contracts and agreements.

- **Scope of Work:** Define what services you will provide.
- **Payment Terms:** Clearly outline the terms of payment.
- **Confidentiality and Liability:** Ensure these aspects are covered to protect both parties.

Consult with a lawyer to ensure these documents are legally sound. Solid contracts not only mitigate risks but also establish trust and professionalism with your clients.

Conclusion

Setting up your fractional COO business requires careful planning and attention to detail. By defining your business structure, registering your business, obtaining the required licenses and permits, setting up your workspace, developing a marketing strategy, building a network, defining your service offerings and pricing structure, and creating contracts and agreements, you'll be well on your way to establishing a successful fractional COO business. This thorough preparation will set a strong foundation for your entrepreneurial journey and help you provide exceptional services to your clients.

Chapter 5: Building Your Client Base

Building a strong client base is essential for the success of your fractional COO business. In this chapter, we will explore the strategies and tactics you can employ to attract and retain clients.

1. Define Your Target Market

Before you can start building your client base, it is important to clearly define your target market. Consider the industries and sectors that can benefit the most from your fractional COO services. Identify the types of businesses that align with your skills, experience, and expertise.

A. Research the Market

Conduct thorough research to understand current market trends, challenges, and opportunities. Stay updated with industry news and developments. Identify potential clients who might need your services. This research will help you tailor your marketing efforts and target the right audience.

B. Identify Ideal Clients

Once you have a clear understanding of the market, identify your ideal clients. These are the businesses that match your target market and can benefit from your expertise. Consider factors such as company size, industry, growth potential, and geographical location.

2. Develop a Marketing Strategy

A well-defined marketing strategy is crucial for attracting clients to your fractional COO business. Here are some strategies you can implement:

A. Create a Professional Website

Having a professional website is essential for establishing your online presence. It serves as a platform to showcase your services, expertise, and success stories. Ensure that your website is visually appealing, user-friendly, and informative.

B. Utilize Content Marketing

Content marketing is an effective way to showcase your expertise and build credibility. Create valuable content such as blog posts, articles, or case studies that address the challenges faced by your target market. Share this content on your website, social media platforms, and relevant industry forums.

C. Leverage Social Media

Social media platforms offer a cost-effective way to reach a large audience. Identify the platforms that are popular among your target market and establish a strong presence. Share informative and engaging content, interact with potential clients, and participate in relevant industry discussions.

D. Attend Industry Events
Attending industry events such as conferences, trade shows, and networking events can provide valuable opportunities to connect with potential clients. Be prepared with your elevator pitch and engage in meaningful conversations. Collect business cards and follow up with potential leads after the event.

3. Build Relationships
Building strong relationships is crucial for client acquisition and retention. Here are some tips for building and nurturing relationships with potential clients:

A. Networking
Networking is a powerful tool for expanding your professional circle. Attend industry events, join professional organizations, and participate in online forums to connect with potential clients. Be genuine, listen actively, and offer value during networking interactions.

B. Referrals and Recommendations
Word-of-mouth referrals and recommendations are highly effective for building trust and credibility. Encourage your satisfied clients to refer your services to their connections. Offer

incentives or discounts to clients who refer you to others.

C. Provide Exceptional Service

Deliver exceptional service to your clients to build strong relationships. Exceed expectations, communicate regularly, and actively listen to their needs. Strive to become a trusted advisor and demonstrate your commitment to their success.

4. Track and Measure Results

Tracking and measuring your marketing efforts is crucial for optimizing your client acquisition strategies. Use analytics tools to monitor website traffic, social media engagement, and lead generation. Regularly review your marketing activities and adjust your strategies based on the data.

Conclusion

Building a robust client base requires a combination of targeted marketing, relationship building, and exceptional service. By defining your target market, developing a comprehensive marketing strategy, and building strong relationships, you can attract and retain clients for your fractional COO business. Stay proactive, adapt to market changes, and continuously strive to deliver the

highest level of service to your clients.

Chapter 6: Providing Exceptional Fractional COO Services

As a fractional COO, providing exceptional services is crucial to not only satisfy your clients' needs but also to position yourself as a trusted and reliable partner. In this chapter, we will explore various strategies and best practices for delivering outstanding fractional COO services.

Understanding Your Clients' Needs

To provide exceptional fractional COO services, it's essential to have a deep understanding of your clients' needs and goals. This begins with effective communication. Take the time to listen and communicate effectively with your clients to grasp their current challenges and desired outcomes. By understanding their pain points, you can tailor your services to address their specific needs effectively.

Building Strong Relationships

Strong relationships are built on trust and understanding. Schedule regular meetings with your clients to discuss their goals, challenges, and expectations. Ask questions that help you gain insight into their business operations and strategic vision. This will allow you to align your efforts with their long-term objectives.

Developing Customized Solutions

Once you have a clear understanding of your clients' needs, it is crucial to develop customized solutions. Each organization is unique, and a one-size-fits-all approach may not work effectively. Analyze your clients' operations and identify areas where you can add value through process improvement, cost reduction, or revenue enhancement. By creating tailored solutions, you can offer targeted and impactful assistance.

Tailoring Your Approach

Consider the specific industry, market conditions, and organizational culture of your client. Use this information to craft strategies that are not only effective but also practical and relevant to their specific situation. For instance, a manufacturing company may need process optimization, while a tech startup might benefit more from strategic scaling advice.

Effective Communication

Communication is key to building strong relationships with your clients. Maintain open lines of communication, ensuring that you regularly update your clients on the progress of their projects or initiatives. Practice active listening to understand your clients' concerns and respond promptly to any queries or requests. By fostering clear and transparent communication, you can build trust and ensure that your clients feel supported throughout the engagement.

Regular Updates and Feedback

Provide regular updates on project milestones, achievements, and any potential issues. Use these updates as opportunities to solicit feedback and adjust your strategies as needed. This continuous feedback loop will help you stay aligned with your clients' expectations and make necessary adjustments in real time.

Providing Regular Reporting

Regular reporting is an essential aspect of providing exceptional fractional COO services. Create customized reports that highlight key metrics, milestones, and achievements. These reports can provide your clients with valuable insights into the impact of your work and help them track progress toward their goals. Regular reporting will not only keep your clients informed but also showcase the value you bring to their organization.

Transparent Reporting

Ensure that your reports are clear, concise, and easy to understand. Use visual aids like charts and graphs to illustrate key points. Transparency in reporting builds trust and demonstrates your commitment to your clients' success.

Collaborative Approach

Adopting a collaborative approach is crucial to providing exceptional fractional COO services. Work closely with your clients' leadership team, employees, and other stakeholders to understand their perspectives, gather feedback, and foster a collaborative environment. By actively involving your clients throughout the process, you can ensure that your services align with their vision and objectives.

Engaging Stakeholders

Engage with various stakeholders to gather diverse perspectives. This collaborative approach helps in developing solutions that are comprehensive and widely accepted within the organization. It also fosters a sense of ownership and commitment among your clients' teams.

Continuous Learning and Professional Development

To provide exceptional fractional COO services, it is essential to stay updated with the latest industry trends and best practices. Invest in continuous learning and professional development opportunities to enhance your expertise. Attend conferences, workshops, and webinars, read industry publications, and network with other professionals in your field. By staying informed, you can offer innovative solutions and stay ahead of the curve.

Keeping Up with Trends

The business landscape is constantly evolving. Regularly update your knowledge base and skill set to adapt to new challenges and opportunities. This proactive approach ensures that you can provide cutting-edge solutions to your clients.

Providing exceptional fractional COO services requires a combination of understanding your clients' needs, developing customized solutions, effective communication, regular reporting, a collaborative approach, and continuous learning. By focusing on these aspects, you can build strong relationships with your clients, deliver valuable results, and establish yourself as a trusted fractional COO in the industry. Always strive for excellence and exceed your clients' expectations to ensure the long-term success of your fractional COO business.

In the next chapter, we'll delve into pricing your fractional COO services effectively, ensuring that your rates reflect the value you provide while remaining competitive. Let's continue to build a thriving and impactful business together.

Chapter 7: Pricing Your Fractional COO Services

Determining the right pricing structure for your fractional COO services is crucial for the success of your business. Not only does it ensure that you are adequately compensated for your expertise and time, but it also attracts the right clients who value your services. In this chapter, we will explore various factors to consider when pricing your fractional COO services.

Factoring in Your Expertise and Experience

Your expertise and experience play a crucial role in determining your pricing. As a fractional COO, you bring a wealth of knowledge and skills to the table, which can significantly impact a company's success. When setting your rates, consider the years of experience you have in your industry, your track record of successful projects, and any specialized knowledge or certifications you possess. Clients will be willing to pay a premium for your expertise and the results you can achieve for their business.

Think about it this way: if you've spent years honing your skills, learning the ins and outs of various industries, and consistently delivering successful outcomes, this makes you a valuable asset. Your experience is not just a number on a resume; it translates into real-world results that can propel a company forward. Highlighting your accomplishments and demonstrating how your expertise can benefit potential clients can justify higher pricing.

Evaluating the Scope of Work

The scope of work involved in each project will vary, and it's important to evaluate and price accordingly. Consider factors such as the size and complexity of the company, the anticipated time commitment, the level of strategic planning required, and the specific tasks and responsibilities involved. This evaluation will help you determine the appropriate pricing structure for each project.

For instance, a small startup might need different services compared to a well-established corporation. The former might require more foundational support, such as setting up operational processes, while the latter might need advanced strategic planning and optimization. Understanding the unique needs of each client and tailoring your services accordingly can help you set a fair and competitive price.

Considering Market Rates

Research and analyze market rates for fractional COO services in your industry. This will give you a benchmark to compare your pricing against and ensure that you are competitive within the market. Look for industry reports, consult with other fractional COOs, and consider joining professional associations or networks to get a better understanding of the prevailing rates.

By understanding what others in your field are charging, you can position yourself appropriately. If you are just starting, you might need to price yourself slightly lower to attract initial clients. However, as you build your portfolio and reputation, you can gradually increase your rates to match or exceed industry standards.

Value-based Pricing

Consider implementing a value-based pricing model, where you align your fees with the value you provide to the client's business. This approach focuses on the outcomes and results you can deliver rather than solely basing your pricing on the number of hours worked. For example, if you can help a client increase their revenue or streamline their operations, the value you bring should be reflected in your pricing.

Value-based pricing can be particularly effective because it shifts the focus from cost to investment. When clients see that your services directly contribute to their bottom line, they are more likely to appreciate the price you set. It's about demonstrating the tangible benefits you bring to their business and aligning your fees with those outcomes.

Flexible Pricing Options

Offering flexibility in your pricing options can attract a broader range of clients. Consider offering tiered pricing packages that cater to different levels of service or customization. This allows clients with various budget constraints to still benefit from your expertise.

For example, you might have a basic package that includes essential services and a premium package that offers more comprehensive support. This way, you can cater to both small businesses with limited budgets and larger companies willing to invest more for extensive services. Flexibility can make your services more accessible and increase your client base.

Transparency and Clear Communication

When discussing pricing with clients, it's important to be transparent and clearly communicate the value you provide. Break down your pricing structure and explain the rationale behind it. This will help clients understand the return on investment they can expect from your services and build trust in your expertise.

Transparency is key to building long-term relationships with clients. When they understand why you charge what you do and see the value in your services, they are more likely to commit and remain loyal. Clear communication can also help manage expectations and prevent misunderstandings down the line.

Revisit and Adjust Pricing Regularly

Pricing is not set in stone, and it's important to regularly revisit and evaluate your pricing strategy. As your experience grows, and as market conditions change, you may need to adjust your prices to ensure they remain fair and reflective of your value. Continuously monitor client feedback, market trends, and industry standards to stay competitive.

Regularly reviewing your pricing strategy allows you to stay adaptable and responsive to changes in the market. It also helps you ensure that your rates accurately reflect the quality and impact of your services.

Conclusion

Pricing your fractional COO services requires careful consideration of factors such as your expertise, the scope of work, market rates, value-based pricing, flexibility, and clear communication. By setting the right pricing structure, you will attract the right clients and ensure the profitability and success of your fractional COO business. Stay proactive, adapt to market changes, and continuously strive to deliver the highest level of service to your clients.

Chapter 8: Managing Your Fractional COO Business

Running a successful fractional Chief Operating Officer (COO) business is no small feat. It demands a blend of strong leadership, sharp operational skills, and strategic foresight. In this chapter, let's dive deep into the essential elements that will help you manage your fractional COO business effectively, ensuring it thrives and grows.

Leadership and Team Management

As a fractional COO, you'll likely find yourself working with a diverse team of professionals. Establishing yourself as a capable leader and fostering a cohesive team environment is crucial. Here are some important aspects to consider:

a. Establish Clear Roles and Responsibilities:

One of the first steps in effective team management is to clearly define each team member's roles and responsibilities. This clarity helps avoid confusion and ensures a smooth workflow. When everyone knows what is expected of them, it sets a productive tone for the work environment.

b. Foster Open Communication:

Encouraging open communication within your team is key. You want everyone to feel comfortable sharing their ideas, concerns, and feedback. Regular team meetings and one-on-one check-ins can go a long way in facilitating this kind of open dialogue.

c. Provide Guidance and Support:

As a leader, your role goes beyond just delegating tasks. It's about providing the necessary guidance and support to help your team members excel. Offer mentorship opportunities, access to professional development resources, and constructive feedback. These efforts will help your team grow and perform at their best.

Financial Management

Effective financial management is the backbone of any successful business, and your fractional COO venture is no exception. Here are some tips to keep your finances in check:

a. Budgeting and Forecasting:

Develop a detailed budget and regularly review it. Keeping track of your income, expenses, and profitability is vital. Use financial forecasting to plan for future growth and to make informed business decisions.

b. Cash Flow Management:

Keeping a close eye on your cash flow is crucial. Ensure you have enough working capital to cover your expenses and investments. Implement strategies to manage your accounts receivable, optimize cash flow, and mitigate any potential financial risks.

c. Bookkeeping and Accounting:

Accurate and up-to-date financial records are essential. Consider hiring a professional bookkeeper or accountant to handle your financial transactions, tax filings, and compliance matters. This professional help can save you time and ensure accuracy.

Operational Efficiency

Delivering high-quality fractional COO services efficiently is essential for client satisfaction and business growth. Here are some strategies to enhance your operational efficiency:

a. Workflow Optimization:

Regularly review and improve your internal processes. Streamlining workflows and reducing redundancies can significantly boost efficiency. Consider automating routine tasks, using project management software, and optimizing communication channels.

b. Performance Tracking:

Set key performance indicators (KPIs) to measure the effectiveness and efficiency of your services. Monitor and analyze these metrics to identify areas for improvement and ensure continuous growth.

c. Continuous Improvement:

Adopt a culture of continuous learning and improvement. Stay updated on industry trends, attend relevant training and conferences, and invest in professional development. Enhancing your skills and knowledge will keep you ahead of the curve.

Client Relationship Management

Building strong relationships with your clients is fundamental to the success and growth of your fractional COO business. Here are some strategies for effective client relationship management:

a. Regular Communication:

Maintain open lines of communication with your clients. Provide regular updates on project progress and address any concerns or questions they may have. Being responsive and proactive in your communication is key.

b. Exceed Expectations:

Always strive to go above and beyond to exceed your clients' expectations. Deliver high-quality work, meet deadlines, and consistently provide value through your services.

c. Seek Feedback:

Regularly seek feedback from your clients to gauge their satisfaction and identify areas for improvement. Act on this feedback to continuously refine your services and better meet your clients' needs.

Conclusion

Managing a fractional COO business requires a blend of effective leadership, sound financial management, operational efficiency, and strong client relationships. By following these strategies, you'll be well-equipped to run and grow your business successfully. Stay focused, adapt to market changes, and always strive for excellence in providing your fractional COO services.

Chapter 9: Scaling Your Fractional COO Business

Scaling your fractional COO business is an exciting but challenging endeavor. As your reputation and client base grow, it's essential to have a solid plan in place for expanding your operations to meet the increasing demands of your clients. This chapter will walk you through key steps to consider when scaling your fractional COO business effectively.

1. Assess Your Current Capacity

Before you begin scaling, it's crucial to evaluate your current capacity and capabilities. Look closely at your existing team, infrastructure, processes, and resources to determine if they can support the anticipated growth. Identify areas that may need improvement or additional investment. For example, you might need more staff, better technology, or streamlined processes to handle an increased workload effectively.

Taking Stock

Conduct a thorough assessment of your current operations. Are your current systems scalable? Can your team handle more clients or more complex projects? This self-evaluation will help you pinpoint any weaknesses that need addressing before you scale up.

2. Define Your Growth Strategy

Developing a clear growth strategy that aligns with your business goals and target market is essential. Decide which areas of your business you want to focus on expanding. This could be increasing the number of clients, broadening your service offerings, or extending your geographical reach. Consider whether you will need to hire additional fractional COOs or support staff to manage the increased workload.

Strategic Planning

Outline a detailed plan that includes short-term and long-term goals. Determine the specific steps you need to take to achieve these goals and the resources required. Having a roadmap will guide your efforts and keep you focused on your objectives.

3. Invest in Infrastructure and Technology

To support your business expansion, invest in the necessary infrastructure and technology. This might include upgrading your software systems, implementing project management tools, or expanding your office space. Ensure that your technology infrastructure is scalable and capable of handling the increased demands of your growing business.

Leveraging Technology

Modern technology can significantly enhance your scalability. Consider adopting cloud-based solutions, automation tools, and other technologies that can streamline operations and improve efficiency. This investment will pay off as you scale and take on more clients.

4. Expand Your Network

Building a strong network is essential for scaling your fractional COO business. Attend industry events, join professional organizations, and participate in networking activities to connect with potential clients and strategic partners. Building relationships with key stakeholders in your industry can lead to new opportunities and referrals for your business.

Networking Strategies

Develop a strategic approach to networking. Identify key events and groups that align with your business goals. Be proactive in seeking out opportunities to meet potential clients and partners, and follow up with contacts to nurture these relationships.

5. Develop Strategic Partnerships

Consider forming strategic partnerships with complementary service providers or consultants in your industry. By collaborating with other experts, you can offer clients a comprehensive suite of services and increase your market reach. Strategic partnerships can also help you access new clients and expand your expertise.

Collaborative Growth

Identify partners who share your values and have a complementary skill set. Work together to create joint offerings that provide added value to clients. These partnerships can be a powerful way to expand your reach and enhance your service portfolio.

6. Streamline Your Processes

As your business grows, it becomes even more important to have efficient and streamlined processes in place. Continually evaluate your internal workflows and identify areas for improvement. Implement automation and standardized procedures wherever possible to maximize productivity and ensure consistent quality of service.

Process Optimization

Regularly review your processes to identify bottlenecks and inefficiencies. Implementing best practices and leveraging technology can help streamline operations and improve overall efficiency. This will ensure that you can scale smoothly without compromising on service quality.

7. Continuously Improve and Innovate

To stay competitive and attract new clients, it's crucial to continuously improve and innovate your service offerings. Stay up-to-date with industry trends, emerging technologies, and best practices. Evaluate client feedback and adjust your services accordingly. By constantly striving to enhance the value you provide, you can differentiate yourself in the marketplace and drive business growth.

Staying Ahead

Make a habit of seeking out new knowledge and skills. Attend workshops, read industry publications, and engage with thought leaders in your field. This continuous improvement mindset will keep you ahead of the competition and ensure your services remain relevant and valuable.

8. Monitor and Measure Success

Set key performance indicators (KPIs) to track the success of your scaling efforts. Regularly monitor and measure important metrics such as revenue growth, client retention rate, and customer satisfaction. These metrics will provide insights into the effectiveness of your growth strategies and help you make data-driven decisions.

Data-Driven Insights

Use data analytics to gain a deeper understanding of your business performance. Analyze trends and patterns to identify areas for improvement and opportunities for growth. Regular monitoring will help you stay on track and make informed decisions.

Conclusion

Scaling your fractional COO business requires careful planning, resource allocation, and strategic decision-making. By assessing your current capacity, defining your growth strategy, investing in infrastructure and technology, expanding your network, developing strategic partnerships, streamlining processes, continuously improving, and monitoring success, you can successfully scale your business to meet the increasing demands of your clients.

Remember, scalability is a journey, and it's important to adapt and evolve your business as you grow. Stay flexible, stay informed, and stay committed to providing exceptional service. With the right strategies in place, you can confidently scale your business and achieve your goals as a fractional COO.

In the next chapter, we will explore how to navigate challenges and sustain success as you scale your business. Let's continue this journey together, ensuring your business not only grows but thrives.

Chapter 10: Navigating Challenges and Sustaining Success

Starting a fractional COO business is an exciting endeavor, but it's important to recognize that challenges will arise along the way. Navigating these challenges and ensuring the long-term success of your business requires resilience, adaptability, and strategic planning. In this chapter, we will discuss common challenges faced by fractional COOs and provide guidance on how to overcome them, as well as strategies for sustaining success in the industry.

1. Overcoming Common Challenges

Running a fractional COO business comes with its own set of unique challenges. By being aware of these challenges and implementing the right strategies, you can overcome them and thrive in your business. Here are some common challenges you may face and tips on how to overcome them:

a. Client Acquisition

One of the biggest challenges for any new fractional COO business is acquiring clients. In a competitive market, it can be difficult to stand out and attract the right clients to your business. To overcome this challenge, it's important to have a clear understanding of your target market and develop a robust marketing strategy.

First, identify your ideal clients and conduct thorough market research to understand their needs, pain points, and buying behaviors. This will enable you to tailor your marketing efforts to effectively reach and resonate with your target audience. Next, develop a professional website that showcases your expertise, experience, and the value you bring to clients. Utilize content marketing to establish yourself as a thought leader in the industry and leverage social media platforms to engage with your target audience.

Networking is also crucial in building relationships with potential clients. Attend industry events, join professional organizations, and actively participate in relevant online communities to expand your network and generate referrals. Lastly, provide exceptional service to your existing clients. Word-of-mouth referrals can be powerful in growing your client base, so always strive to exceed client expectations and deliver exceptional results.

b. Managing Client Expectations

Another challenge faced by fractional COOs is managing client expectations. As a fractional COO, you will be working closely with clients to drive operational efficiency and improve processes. It's important to set realistic expectations from the beginning and continuously communicate with your clients to ensure alignment.

Clearly define the scope of work and deliverables for each project or engagement. Establish key performance indicators (KPIs) and regularly provide progress reports to keep clients informed about the progress and results achieved. Maintaining transparent and open communication channels is essential in managing client expectations. Encourage clients to provide feedback and address any concerns or issues promptly. By keeping the lines of communication open, you can prevent misunderstandings and build stronger relationships with your clients.

c. Dealing with Resistance to Change

Implementing change within an organization can be met with resistance from employees and stakeholders. As a fractional COO, part of your role is to navigate and facilitate change within the client's organization. This can be a challenging task, but with the right strategies, you can help clients overcome resistance to change.

Start by clearly communicating the need for change and the benefits it will bring to the organization. Develop a comprehensive change management plan that includes stakeholder engagement, communication strategies, and training programs to effectively address resistance and ensure a smooth transition. Involve key stakeholders in the decision-making process and seek their input and feedback. By involving them from the start, you can help create a sense of ownership and buy-in for the proposed changes. Continuous education and communication are also key to overcoming resistance to change. Provide regular updates on the progress of the change initiatives and communicate the positive impact of the changes on the organization.

2. Sustaining Success

Sustaining success in the fractional COO business requires ongoing commitment, continuous improvement, and adaptability. Here are some strategies to help you sustain success in the long term:

a. Stay Ahead of Industry Trends

The business landscape is constantly evolving, and it's important to stay up to date with the latest trends and best practices in your industry. Continuously invest in your professional development by attending industry conferences, workshops, and webinars. Stay connected with thought leaders and stay informed about emerging trends that can impact your clients' businesses.

b. Foster Client Relationships

Building strong relationships with your clients is crucial for sustaining success. Regularly communicate with your clients, seek feedback, and proactively identify opportunities for improvement. Exceed their expectations by consistently delivering high-quality work and demonstrating your commitment to their success. Additionally, maintain a customer relationship management (CRM) system to track client interactions, preferences, and future opportunities. This will help you stay organized and proactively engage with your clients.

c. Expand Your Service Offerings

As your business grows, consider expanding your service offerings to meet the evolving needs of your clients. Conduct market research to identify new opportunities and assess the feasibility of expanding into related areas. This can include offering additional consulting services, such as organizational development or strategic planning, or specializing in specific industries or niches. By diversifying your service offerings, you can attract a wider range of clients and increase your revenue streams, thus ensuring the long-term sustainability of your business.

d. Focus on Continuous Improvement

Never settle for mediocrity. Continuously seek ways to improve your service delivery, operational efficiency, and client satisfaction. Regularly review and analyze client feedback to identify areas for improvement and implement necessary changes. Invest in your own professional development by acquiring new skills, certifications, or qualifications. This will enhance your expertise and credibility, allowing you to offer additional value to your clients.

e. Monitor Key Performance Indicators (KPIs)

Establish key performance indicators (KPIs) to track the success and profitability of your fractional COO business. Regularly monitor and analyze these KPIs to gain insights into your business operations and make data-driven decisions. Track metrics such as client retention rates, revenue growth, client satisfaction scores, and project profitability. This will help you identify areas of strength and areas that need improvement, allowing you to make informed decisions to sustain and grow your business.

Conclusion

Navigating challenges and sustaining success in the fractional COO business requires adaptability, continuous learning, and a customer-centric mindset. By overcoming common challenges, staying ahead of industry trends, fostering client relationships, expanding service offerings, focusing on continuous improvement, and monitoring key performance indicators, you can position your fractional COO business for long-term success. Remember, success is not a destination but an ongoing journey of growth and improvement.

www.ingramcontent.com/pod-product-compliance
Lightning Source LLC
Chambersburg PA
CBHW070426240526
45472CB00020B/1472